Contributing Authors

Alexandra Jarrett

Alicia BigCanoe

Alyson Bear

Ashley Richard

Aura

Brenda Royal

Casey Rhae Desjarlais

Charlene Hellson

Chief Lady Bird

Diana Hellson

Destiny Rae

Erica Lugt

Evelyn Pakinewatik

Helen Oro

Inuk (@Inuk360)

kivvaq (Nikita Larter)

Jacey Firth-Hagen

Jade Roberts

Janelle Pewapsconias

Kaniehtiio Horn

Karalyn Menicoche

Kaya Joan

Kluane Adamek

Lila May Erasmus

Magdalena Kelly

Michelle Malla

Mika Lafond

Nicole Ineese-Nash

Nigit'stil Norbert

Peyton Straker

Sadie-Phoenix Lavoie

Wentanoron Ariana Roundpoint

Cover Art

Aura

Chief Lady Bird

asinnajaq (Isabella Weetaluktuk)

Graphic Design

kivvaq (Nikita Larter)

Edgar Gonzalez-Rodriguez

Project Coordinator

Kayla Rosteski-Merasty

Project Support

Jennifer Corriero

Mitch Holmes

Silvia Olteanu

This project is dedicated to Indigenous youth. It is inspired
by Nigit'stil Norbert (Director of our Connected North
Youth Leadership Fund based in Yellowknife, Northwest
Territories) and Karalyn Menicoche (Connected North
Indigenous Student Leader from Deh Gah Got'ie Koe' (Fort
Providence), Northwest Territories) who shared reflections
on the experiences of Indigenous students and the need for
role models. The title for this first book, which will be part
of an anthology, is *Three Sisters Soup for the Spirit.*
The name of the book was envisioned by Chief Lady
Bird and Aura over a lunch conversation with our
TakingITGlobal Executive Director during Indigenous
Fashion Week 2018.

We would like to acknowledge the land, the families
and ancestors of all our contributing authors, artists and
TakingITGlobal team members who have contributed to
this project.

If you could provide a message to the younger version of yourself to get through school, life, and challenging circumstances, what would you say?

This book includes a compilation of poetry, short stories, and visual art from First Nations, Métis and Inuit Women. The submissions aim to inspire youth in overcoming challenges with themes around passion, independant voice, and joy. The project is dedicated to Indigenous high school students who are part of the TakingITGlobal's Connected North program by featuring the power of creativity through different role models and promoting mental health.

TakingITGlobal is one of the world's leading networks of young people; learning about, engaging with, and working towards tackling local and global challenges. *Connected North* fosters student engagement and enhanced education outcomes in remote Indigenous communities. This leading edge program delivers immersive and interactive education services, through Cisco's high definition, two-way TelePresence video technology. The goal is to provide students and teachers with access to content that is engaging and innovative, with the hope of increasing feelings of empowerment in school and in life.

As you take the time to read through the different
contributions, we encourage you to make space for your own
self care and personal reflections. Some of the content may
bring up different emotions related to your own experiences.
It might help to have some blank paper and a pencil ready
to express your own thoughts or consider having a reading
group with trusted friends so that you can talk to someone
about your ideas, memories and hopes for the future. If you
are going through something very difficult, it might also
help to speak with an elder, councillor or community worker
depending on what might be available to you.

Sincerely,

Kayla Rosteski-Merasty

Nigit'stil Norbert

Jennifer Corriero

Contents

A Disaster Occurred

By Charlene Hellson *(Home: Calgary, AB | Current: Vancouver, BC)*

A disaster occurred. It felt unreal as it happened but in the aftermath it was too real...her thoughts, feelings, and sensations...scattered and torn like the clothes she wanted to burn. In spite of the shock she made the call. The response was immediate, and the support compassionate, but soon she was home alone with nightmares, flashbacks, and anxiety attacks that left her breathless on the floor. Help was on the way, but a long way off.

While she waited her home became a prison surrounded by a razor wire fence of silence. Frustration, confusion, helplessness fuelled loss of control followed by loss of friends, family, job, home, and self. With no one to hear the pain firing the rage, no one to help her mend the fabric of her life, no one to tell her 'it's not your fault' self-blame made its way from her head through her heart and settled into her core. Shame became the cloak she wore to hide from a world that did not believe her, and instead dismissed, diagnosed, and drugged her. She's coping, self-medicating, and hoping. She's waiting...waiting for someone to connect, for someone to help her unlock the gate, remove the cloak, and believe her.

Mental Health Awareness

By Alyson Bear (Tatanka-ska-wi) *(Whitecap Dakota First Nation)*

For me I was not always aware of how much of my personal well-being had so much to do with what I was doing in life. Taking care of yourself, putting yourself first is not always easy and especially as a mother, you have to make sure you are taking care of yourself if you are even going to have anything to give to your children. They need you at your best, not your worst and that is something we need to fully understand as parents. It is better to make it easier on people then harder and not be so hard on ourselves. The world already does a very good job at doing that for us.

Everywhere we go no matter where we look and now with the power of technology we are totally plugged into it 24/7, draining our energy. Images, ads, subliminal messages telling us we are not good enough. Always being told how to look, what to eat, who to be, since the get go, since we came out of the womb. It is plastered on billboards, on magazines in the grocery stores, on the television, movies, commercials ads everywhere we look, consumerism is consuming us, in this capitalistic society we live in. We are literally marinated in Eurocentric Worldviews. That is also why everybody seems to be adopting so much of the oppressor's worldviews and their ways to handle problems and life.

Trauma and Tragedy come natural with life and unfortunately for many

Indigenous peoples it is life for us on the regular. It seems almost foreign to live life without trauma and tragedy. We have to try and get through what seems like barrier after barrier to get to any safe or comfortable places in this world, and society. If you could have a degree in lived experience I know many Indigenous peoples who would have their masters and phD's. Is it not life experience who makes us who we are?

That is why when we are going from one experience to another not actually healing it is affecting us and running us down and while we consume and consume, things that are not healthy for us and our well-being. Therefore, we are not taking care of one another and no wonder why mental illness on the rise. The entire world is out of balance right now with climate change, the massive amount of pollution happening to Mother Earth, the ocean, atmosphere, endangered species on the rise, and more and more issues and mental issues within society itself. Yet so many people continue to live in denial and choose the oppressor's way of life.

There is a suicide crisis happening in Indigenous communities.
There are MMIWG still being stolen from us every single day. They are still taking our children, and putting them into their system.
The overrepresentation of Indigenous men, women and youth incarcerated continues to rise. The Justice for Colton Boushie movement is happening and it continues to show on its face that racism is alive and well in our communities and for some reason the justice system has never been on our side.

It is hard to live in a society that is trying to eliminate your people and assimilate your people or make your people self-destruct, always pointing the finger and saying hey you guys are doing this to yourselves. Always convincing you that you are not good enough for that job or good enough for this world. A feeling of complete hopelessness a feeling I have felt before.

Mental illness is real and we need to take care of ourselves so we can take care of each other. It is up to us to show the future there is a good way to live life and it comes from letting go of a lot of comfort zones and things we think we know and embracing who we truly are and walking that path less taken to show those to come a better way. There is a lot of work to be done but not all is hopeless is what we need to remember, and we are never alone when we walk with the prayers of our ancestors. Resilient are my people.

The Darkness

By Wentanoron Ariana Roundpoint

(Akwesasne, Ontario)

It was a blanket,

Not the warm one that kept you alive in the winter,

But the cool one that embraced you when danger came forth.

It was a voice,

Not the one who told you to jump,

But the one who reminded you of what there was to live for.

It was a hand,

Not the one that let go,

But the one that held on through the storm.

It was a reminder,

Not of what to fear,

But of what to embrace and recognize.

It was a battle cry,

Not for pain, suffering, and loneliness,

But for the strong, the resilient, the unforgetting.

It was a shield,

Not from those who would harm,

But those who sought to diminish a light, a spark, a fire.

This Darkness was the Universe.

A place where all dwelled,

Where time and direction meant nothing,

Where the darkness was everywhere and nowhere,

Where fear had no foothold.

This Darkness dwells within each of us.

It is not malicious.

It is there to be the mother to us all.

It is there to remind us that the darkness is needed,

To see even the brightest star.

This Darkness was all of us,

And none of us.

This Darkness is our core,

And our armour.

This Darkness is the light at the end of the tunnel.

This Darkness is our hope.

Look up.

Look out.

Look beyond.

You will see this Darkness.

You will feel this Darkness.

You will become this Darkness.

Forever Woman: A Grandmother's Love

By Ashley Richard

(Home: Pine Creek First Nation &

Camperville, MB | Current: Winnipeg, MB)

I clearly remember the moment as if it were yesterday. The sun is setting on a warm summer evening, and wind blows through the windows of the taxi and hits my face in the backseat. We're driving fast down the highway. But I'm comfortable. I'm content. I look up at the woman beside me and I see my grandmothers face. She beams down at me and in that moment my little heart is filled with so much love that I feel it may burst. I'm too young to realize that this is the only time in my life I will ever feel this way. In this moment, I know I can ask her anything.

"Grandma, what does my spirit name mean?"

"My girl, it means you're going to grow up to be a powerful woman – even more powerful than me."

I awoke to the sound of the drum

The sun spilled into the room

I knew my grandmother's time had come

With every beat I felt time move faster

I held her hand and watched her take her last breath

The drum slowed and eventually silenced

And with the last beat went any will I had to create a life path of my own.

"Even more powerful than me", a now laughable feat

I will hate every minute of this life without her

There were days I would look up at the sky and scream at it to fall

Just so I could comfort my skin in the hot embers of chaos

Anything to wash away the agony of her absence

Freely giving sacred parts of mind, body, and spirit

Because the lonely invent love where it doesn't really exist

Beaten and broken down I looked at my reflection in the mirror

Lifeless eyes stared back at me

Broken and bruised

I lifted my hand to feel the bruises and cuts along my face

My mind's eye formed a miserable smirk

The enemy of our ancestors was winning

I was beaten beyond recognition

Beaten by an addiction to destruction

Forever Woman

A powerful woman

My grandmother's life and legacy

Me?

It was more than a decade before, but I recognized the feeling of that sun. It was the same sun. I opened my eyes expecting to be back in the taxi, but I found myself in my bedroom. Where was she? I looked over to the door and saw it slowly slide open. First, I saw her head poke in, then slowly the rest of her came in through the door way. I was so happy to see her but I couldn't talk for some reason. She trailed across the room and climbed into the bed next to me. She sat up and put my head in her lap and I felt the warmth of her body right next to mine. Still, I stayed silent.

"My girl, what's wrong?"

I opened my mouth to tell her everything that I felt, but all that came out was

"Grandma, I just miss you so much."

I cried for hours while she stroked my hair. There was no need for any other words. I just needed to feel her here and to know that she was with me, and here she was. I buried my face in tears and never wanted her to leave again, but I knew she had to.

I opened my eyes to feel a heart full of love

Winters had gone by and I felt like I had forgotten what it was like

Forgotten what it was like to value life

Forgotten what it was like to feel love

To feel anything

Forever Woman

A powerful woman

My grandmother's life and legacy

Me.

Broken and Afraid

By Sadie-Phoenix Lavoie *(Sagkeeng Anishinaabe Nation)*

Alone in a world full of lost souls

Obsessed with ignoring the past

Floating through time like ghouls

Reckless memories erased so fast

Walking around up to no good

You used to be a teacher's pet

But in this haunted neighbourhood

You get sucked up if you let it

Kicked out, a constant runaway

Result of the hurt and cultural emptiness

Looking for another way

Out of this traumatic mess

Used, abused and victimized

My spirit collected moon dust

There from the stars, I realised

A new journey was a must.

High and Low, I searched far and wide

For the pieces I lost at night

To help me come to the bright side

Through the lens of my inner sight

Missing pieces bound to occur

A little taken from him

Extra given from her

Regardless, my light would never dim

Damaged but bandaged with ceremony

The sounds of language are so beautiful

Finally the full picture I could see

Living life then became delightful

I'm still me with more enlightened experiences

I guess I just needed to be upgraded

Learn to break systemic walls and racist fences

Reason my people stay faded

Awaken United and Proud

The lighting of the 8th Fire all around

By the missing spark I found

Resurgence and revitalization are now desired.

Truth and Reconciliation so we can heal

The wrongs of genocide will forever be a stain

But no longer our burden to feel

So rest assured injustice won't remain.

Pink Earth Woman

By Casey Rhae Desjarlais

(Home: Treaty 4 & Treaty 6 Territories

& Saskatoon, SK | Current: Coast Salish Territory, BC)

I put on my regalia

& I am whole again.

My ancestors are with me

& I feel content.

I hear

the drums, the heartbeat of Mother Earth

& I am safe.

The vibrations of my feet hitting the

ground reminds me of where I come from, the land.

& I am home again.

It's Not Depression, It's a Side Effect of Oppression

By Casey Rhae Desjarlais

(Home: Treaty 4 & Treaty 6 Territories & Saskatoon, SK

Current: Coast Salish Territory, BC)

Bear with me, I haven't left the house in days. My stomach turns as the sunlight touches my golden skin. My mouth is dry but my eyes are watering.

The smell of pine and dust. Green and blue hues and morning dew.

It took 2 strong cups of coffee but I'm awake. I burn some sage & hold myself.

The smoke takes me back in time, I close my eyes. I can see now.

The children are laughing, blueberry stained lips. The echoing sound of drumming is coming from over the hill. The glistening water captures my soul as Grandmother hums silently beside me. The ground under my feet is cool and I can feel the vibrations of her breath. I whisper to the wind, "I'm back".

I open my eyes. The sun on my face is refreshing. I take a sip & breathe.. I think I'll stay out of bed today.

I've got work to do.

Mother's Milk

By Nigit'stil Norbert

(Gwich'ya Gwich'in & Yellowknife, NT)

Fat dripping.

That beautiful light in the Delta.

Gwich'in and Inuvialuit country.

My heart aches for your lands and waters that fill my womb with nectar.

My bones are sore and need the nourishment from animals blood and

bones and meat and flesh.

Fresh fish fat dripping into my mouth.

Dripping in that beautiful light in the Delta.

Sisters

By Chief Lady Bird *(Home: Rama First Nation &*

Moose Deer Point First Nation | Current: Tkaronto)

A sister is a beacon

Light

That draws my frail moth body to her

Light

That unearths my truth

Light

That pulls me from darkness.

I am a vessel

Carrying dirty water

Tainted by our colonizers

Washing their hands with my sacredness.

But my sister is also a vessel.

She carries dirty water

Tainted by systemic violence

And

Unconsented acts of consumption.

Just like me.

Together we pour our dirty water into a new vessel and Suddenly,

There seems to be less dirt.

Together we stand in solidarity.

Together we stand with strength.

Decolonial monuments of feminine strength in numbers

Weathered by the wind,

We stay rooted.

Together we give our offerings

And hold our tobacco to the water,

Arms outstretched, leaning as far as we can

Despite the heaviness of the bodies

Slung over our shoulders like back packs.

Every day

We carry our lost sisters

Livegivers

Who lost their lives at the hands of hatred

And contempt for their kind spirits

That was taught by a country

That never saw their worth.

Every day

We carry the children

Who had Christianity beat into them

To "save" their heathen souls

That didn't walk on Jesus's path

Because their teacher was the Earth

And everything that exists between the land and the sky.

Every day

We carry our ancestors

And all of their teachings

That were nearly forgotten

Because the settler mentality

Told us to be ashamed of them.

Every day

We carry our brothers and sisters

Who wrestle with addiction.

Alcohol runs through their veins

As they struggle to wake up every morning

And face the streets they call home...

A life of urban survival that was forced upon them.

Every day

We carry each other

Dreamers with good intentions

That extend far beyond our own needs

Carrying the change that will help

The next seven generations

With the reclamation of our languages and traditions.

Our backs strain from the tension

But our bones don't break.

We share the weight of these burdens that each of us are born with.

We have passed the genocidal magnus.

Our existence is pure survival.

Our existence is pure love.

A sweetgrass braid,

mushkiikii for our nation.

When it all feels like too much,

I reach out and take my sister's hand.

She reminds me of my teachings:

To walk with love,

To speak with wisdom,

To live my truth,

To create with honesty,

To walk through creation with humility,

To honour life's balance with respect,

To wake up every morning and feel brave.

I am a beacon

Light

That draws my sister's frail moth body to me

Light

That unearths her truth

Light

That pulls her from darkness.

Watching the world die

While you just sat

Whats up with that?!

Give your head a shake

We have a lot at stake

The privileged race can no longer take

It's time to accept this simple reality

Coming from a place of rationality

Racism has gotten to extreme severity

It's time for you to look in the mirror

And face your biggest fear

It's alright to shed a tear

I am here

One the other side of this great divide.

Freedom (Excerpt)

By Diana Hellson (Mamarudegyal MTHC)

(Home: Calgary, AB | Current: Burnaby, BC)

One Woman,

Lasting Love and Loving Last,

Lasting like Eternal Past

She Screams out.

Born under the Red Moon

She Seeketh

Strength without Limits

Tangible,

Intangible,

Unmanageable.

Free.

You Will Bring Change

By Helen Oro *(Pelican Lake First Nation, Treaty 6 Territory)*

The hopeless empty feeling of being alone will pass, it won't last long. Abandoned, given up, tossed away are thoughts that will fill your mind as you grow, triggers of being hurt and left will linger. If only I can help you see who you will become one day, if only I could show you what happiness you will give to others. You will give hope and inspire others to believe in themselves. You will bring change and save lives with your words and actions. If only I could help you see sooner the light that shines within. You're not alone, try your best, things get better, get through the day even if you feel like it's impossible tomorrow is a new day and it's up to you how that tomorrow feels. Your dreams will become reality, and that reality will become a passion. That light within will shine so bright everyone will feel the warmth.

Dream HUGE

By Inuk (aka: Brendalynn Inuk Trennert) *(@Inuk360)*

YOU are not only a beautiful and intelligent person, but you will be more resilient than you could ever imagine. You must NEVER give up, stand your ground and be true to your very own dreams, ethics, and beliefs. You keep dreaming HUGE and then working so hard that you never knew how hard you would have to work to live each of your dreams. I would tell my younger self, you do NOT have to "fit in" and it IS very okay to be different. I would tell my young self when someone you like or you think you love, they will not pressure you in to you doing things, like smoking, drinking or sex. I am so very proud that you never became a dope smoker and said good bye to alcohol by 22 years old; thank you - young self, you saved our life.

I would look me in the eye's with understanding eye's and a compassionate heart and tell Inuk, you will be loved for you, don't confuse sex with love. I would tell my young self, life is not going to be easy but it will be worth living so do not give up. It is okay to say out loud to others, that you are not okay and need to talk with someone, do not keep your smile on your face as the pain will eat you from the inside out. I would tell my young self so many things but most of all I would hug the shit out of her and say to her, what an amazing life you will build, so keep moving forward, never regretting your life choices and never give up.

How has art impacted my life:

Wow! By the time I was 22 years old, I knew I was born to be a caribou hair tufter, and had decided that i would become the best tufter I could be, and so I did. I have now traveled around the world a couple of times to teach, demonstrate, and sell my caribou hair tuftings. By the age of 25, I was well on my way to being and called a Master Tufter. It is not easy becoming the best in your chosen field, and even harder to maintain your well-earned title, but it will definitely be worth the work.

My art is the air I breathe, the threads I sew are the blood to my life and the people I teach are the legacy I will leave this world with.

My biggest message to youth IS: dream HUGE, then work work work and work till you live each of your dreams. Stay sober, drug free, a violence free ... LIFE IS A GIFT, do not waste it on alcohol, cigarettes or drugs. Finally, leave the world in better shape than when you entered it ... That is what I am doing.

Love,

Inuk

Be Unapologetically You

By Jade Roberts *(Home: Treaty 6 & La Ronge | Current: Saskatoon, SK)*

Life is hard, but we wouldn't be who we are without our struggles. Understand that there is always someone cheering you on, and when you feel like there isn't, that's when you need to be your own cheerleader. I don't claim to know everything about life, and I get that everyone has their own story. However, I have been through my fair share of struggles and different experiences. Here are a few things I wish I would have known a litter sooner.

1. Be unapologetically you. There is no one else like you in this world, so don't give the world a watered down version of yourself; we want the real you. Speak your mind, state your opinions, allow yourself to be open. Never fear being yourself; the people who truly love you, love you because you are who you are, and those are the people who matter.

2. You are never stuck. Often times we feel like we are stuck where we are so we limit ourselves. Stop doing that! You can be anything, you can do anything, and you can go anywhere. Tell yourself everyday what you aspire to be, what you hope to do, and where you want to go. Remember that everything is a mindset, so keep a positive one and manifest what you want. Eventually you'll find yourself becoming free of the situation in which you thought you were stuck. Be patient with yourself during these times.

3. Be healthy: physically, emotionally, mentally, and spiritually. We are never truly a whole person until we fulfill each one of these aspects of ourselves. Think of yourself as four different pieces: physical, emotional, mental, and spiritual. If you are missing one of your pieces, you're not going to feel your best. Take time each day to do something that makes each piece of you healthy, whatever that is, you decide.

4. Set goals. If you don't have something to work towards then you are not bettering yourself.Set small goals, set big goals. Dream up whatever you want and take baby steps to get there. It's easy to set a goal, but the only way it's going to work is if you do. Remind yourself that you need to put in the work to reach your goals, and if that means being selfish once in a while then that's okay. Don't be too hard on yourself.

5. Be kind. How you treat others is a reflection of how you feel about yourself. Accept everyone for who they are, treat everyone with respect, and always be kind. Most importantly, be kind to yourself. When you can learn to do this, you'll realize that loving yourself results in being able to love others.

You Are No Less Cree Than Me

By Janelle Pewapsconias *(@ecoaborijanelle)*

(Little Pine First Nation)

City children

Feral, concrete, and Cree

Mouths salivating

Dripping with "ehh"'s and "ahh"'s

In deep parts of Nehiyaw tongues

Running past and fast

Beside city busses

Big as buffalo

You are no less Cree than me

We Carry This World For You

By Janelle Pewapsconias *(@ecoaborijanelle)*

(Little Pine First Nation)

I carry this world for you

Because

You've been a prayer

On ancestors lips

Pressed down in syllables

And rhythms

In the very vibration of this world

You are energy

Creation

Gifts to all of us

Our connection

Our way back

Our long time coming

Sovereign in your body

Your waterways bring life

Your laughter lifts us up

I know it is you

I feel it

You came in riding wind currents

Like a change in temperature

Clouds breathing in

Calm before the rush of your storm

You make the grasses bow

Even aspens tremble differently

See, you've been the prayer

On ancestors lips

Even as a baby

You articulate thunder

Booming loudly

Each time you cried

Your time is now, young one

You bring change

Until you are ready

We carry this world for you

Dear Little Pine Needles,

By Kaniehtiio Horn *(Mohawk, Kanienkehaka Bear Clan from Kahnawake)*

You are unique. You are special. You are important. You are loved.

We all have unique gifts that we bring into the world when we are born. These gifts were passed down from our relatives and ancestors, like pine needles that fall from the tree onto the ground they are absorbed back into the earth to continue the cycle of life. My Ma told us that inside each one of us we have a spark, a tiny flame that is our spirit and it is our responsibility to nurture that little flame by always looking after our mind and body.

I was raised from birth with a very strong sense of responsibility to my people and my community. Watching my older sisters succeed in the careers they chose, I put a lot of pressure on myself to not totally suck at whatever I decided to do.

I tried my best to always remember that tiny little flame.

When we are given our names, one thing the community is reminded of is the responsibility they have to recognize our gifts and to help us reach our full potential. Imagine your family, good friends and community as a bright, warm, roaring fire. Without you and your little flame that fire wouldn't be as bright. These are the people that use their tiny flames to help light your path while also keeping you warm and toasty. They can be the family you were born into or the family you create, the important thing is they make you feel good.

I have six older sisters, three Kanienkehaka sisters through my mother and three through my father. My father is not Indigenous, although his daughters before me had an Ojibwe mom, so they're all half (but whole) like me. I have never felt like I totally fit in anywhere but I was lucky to grow up with these amazing examples in my life; my loving parents, even though they were divorced, and six big sisters. They always encouraged me to be myself, no matter how 'out there' that was, the weirder the better. They'd dress me up and get me to sing to them and to this day my absolute favourite thing in the world is to make the people I love laugh.

Eventually I ended up in theatre school and I have a vivid memory of driving on a road in Kahnawake with my mother when I was about 17. I'm not sure where we were coming from, maybe just the post-office and back home, but I remember asking her a question that had been on my mind;

"How does being an actor help my people?"

"You'll figure it out.", she answered.

All of my instincts growing up, the encouragement and help from my family, everything that made me happy brought me to this place in my life. I was actually becoming an actor, I was exactly where I wanted to be, but I was still unsure how I fit in. For this moment in my life I had demeaned the path I had taken, as if it wasn't the correct one. Why? I don't know I guess maybe because I wasn't on the front lines delivering babies or running for office, I couldn't see anything important with where I ended up.

I continued my journey eventually graduating theatre school and working as a professional. I still didn't understand what the heck it was that was so special about being an actor. I felt like it was such a selfish career path but it really was all I wanted to do. Through my journey I found other sparks that helped my flame flicker brighter, and also some that dimmed my little flame. I learned those flame-dimmers aren't the people who help guide you on your path.

One day it finally hit me. I am a story teller. Storytellers are important. Everyone has stories. From then on I have felt a sense of purpose and fulfillment, but this didn't happen over night. It was a journey I took, armed with all of the tools and knowledge passed down from my family and ancestors. I was confident that if I cared for the little flame inside me that lights my path then I will end up exactly where I am supposed to be.

So Little Pine Needles, you have a flame inside of you too. A flame passed down from your relatives and the people before you. Look after your mind and steer clear of flame-dimmers, people or things that don't help you glow bright. Don't let anyone, including yourself, demean the things that make you happy. Look after your body, so you can be healthy and always at your full potential. Be open, take chances and experience as much as you can, because that little flame needs oxygen to stay flickering.

Look after these three things; your mind, your body and your little flame spirit so that you too can eventually be an old pine needle with a wealth of knowledge. You will go back into the ground and eventually other Little Pine Needles will be sprouting up on the trees, but they wouldn't ever have gotten there without you.

You are unique. You are special. You are important. You are loved.

Once You Express Yourself, Good Things Always Follow

By Karalyn Menicoche *(Deh Gah Got'ie Koe' (Fort Providence), NT)*

Live your life as you are aiming to please your inner intuitions, through things that make you feel happy and successful. It is always beneficial to practice and use your culture traditions to help preserve your identity and to have that gain in life through knowing who you are.

This can also go for a non-Indigenous person, do not feel reluctant or discouraged to learn or practice another culture, as long as you being mindful and respectful. In my culture we are always happy to tell of our Dene ways, as we see it as building relationships and special bonds with one another.

Also learning to express yourself and learning to use your voice as a tool to help spread goodness, through passion and love, you will be amazed on how many people you will naturally attract. To be able to find your passion where you can use your greatest capabilities to its advantage and be that difference in this world, is what I would tell any young person.

Learning to accept and not judge is a big barrier to overcome. One tactic that helped me when I was a teen was going to the school counsellor on my own will. I was taught that if something doesn't feel right or is bothering me "talk about it, don't hold it in." This will then naturally open your senses and good ways that helps for understanding and of course to expand your learning capabilities. This ties into the process of "Trust", to open your heart to trust people or things even though you experience something that was wrong. This is a way to help yourself grow from those experiences, because it's through the darkest moments we will find our greatest gifts.

Always be proud of who you are and where you come from. Our ancestors paved a good path for us to follow and to learn from. Spend time listening to stories from our elders, even if it is spoken in your Indigenous language, you will always remember the moments and treasure those special times. Take the time to learn your mother tongue, we all have it in our blood, it is just the matter of practicing and giving it time, and you will learn it. I am proud to say I am 30% fluent in my Dene language and practice every day with my young child. Your language is something that no one can ever take away from you, and to speak your language makes so much richer as an Indigenous person.

To take the time and reflect on my personal life and write this passage of my own, I am hoping to inspire our people to strive to be the best they can be. Do not be afraid to make mistakes, take it as a learning curve and use it to the best of your abilities. Everything happens for a reason, know that and in the end you will be able to conquer all obstacles that come your way!

Wishing you all the greatest journey. Mahsi cho.

Growth

By Kaya Joan *(Tkaronto)*

Someday You Will Stand Upon Our Shoulders

By Lila May Erasmus *(Home: Whitehorse, YK | Current: Yellowknife, NT)*

As parents we want only the best for our children. We struggle through life hoping that everything we do will make a difference in yours. We sacrifice, we endure, we fall and we get back up again for you: knowing that someday you will stand upon our shoulders and see further than we were ever able to. These words of wisdom, just for you:

1. Adults do not know everything: Adults are just learning, the same as you are just learning...it's weird, I know. I always thought that when I become an adult, I will know how to deal with everything...nope, not true!! Mistakes are a part of life no matter how old you get: You will grow because of them and you will never know everything, but you will always be learning and that's a good thing.

2. Change is good: Know that nothing stays the same and never will. Whether you are happy, content, sad or angry: it will not stay that way. Sometimes you will be so happy you will NEVER want it to change, but know that it will change, shift, grow and yes, possibly come to an end: so be grateful for your blessings as they happen. Sometimes you will be so sad that you will want it to change NOW: it may not happen when you want it to but know that it will. Change can be uncomfortable because you do not know what is on the other side. But you will see that once you get to the other side, it will be ok, you may even better because of it.

3. Don't take life too seriously: It is so important for you to know, that it will be ok no matter what. Learn to laugh at yourself and learn to laugh at life. Be good to people, work hard and relax. Someday you will discover that it is ok to do nothing at all, goof off, and take a sick day when you are not really sick: It is good to laugh, it is good to cry. Find your passion and work hard to achieve your goals but have fun while you are doing it: That is important.

4. Enjoy your own company: There will be times when you will feel so alone, like you do not have a friend in the world. Sometimes you may even feel like the whole world is against you: It is sad, I know, but true. When you learn to love yourself, you will discover that others will want to be around you. So weird, hey: you are going to think "where were they when I needed someone to love me"…well, my little one, they were always there but it is hard to see love when you don't feel love. But, if you love yourself and enjoy your own company, you will never be without a friend who is wonderfully funny, intelligent, kind and generous.

5. Define yourself: Bad things will happen to you no matter how good you try to be and not everyone is going to love you no matter how much you try to please them. Sad as it is, you will feel this but know you will overcome these hurts. Even though, at the times, you may feel like the hurt will never go away, you are stronger than you think. Someday, you will come to understand your own power and when that happens you will no longer allow others to take it from you. The love and kindness of others who believe in you, your friends, family, ancestors, Creator, let those words be the constant whisper of encouragement in your ear that supports you to define your own destiny!

6. Trust your Creator: Creator made all of the most beautiful things in the world and of all those things he created, he also thought to create YOU! He has a plan for you and he wants you to win. He will teach you and he will guide you: not always in ways you agree with but if you listen carefully with love and trust in your heart, you will see how kind and generous he is: you will see how much he loves you! My babies, you will grow to become stronger than you ever dreamed possible; you will live a good life full of family and friends that will love you more than their words can ever express. You are beautiful, you are loved, you are protected and you are destined for greatness!!

With love, xoxo

You Can Handle Most Anything

By Magdalena Kelly *(Home: Le'qamel First Nation (sto:lo nation) Current: Vancouver, BC)*

You are young and have the whole world ahead of you, you are bright eyed and ready for whatever adventure comes your way and that is a beautiful thing! One thing that I really would love to tell you is that no matter who tries to put their problems onto you, they are their issues. People may come into your life and see your openness and try to take advantage of that innocence, but don't you worry, you are strong and you can handle a lot. This is not to disregard your feelings however, as your feelings are very valid and important, but I am just letting you know that you can handle most anything that comes your way.

No matter what has been told to you, or not matter who has shushed you or not allowed you to speak your mind, what you have to say and how you feel is important! You are important! There will be a lot of people in the future that will come to depend on you so your strength is something that is needed in this world, don't ever let anyone tell you any different! That is your gift to the world and something that not everyone is capable of. It makes you unique and you will realize one day that it is your gift and you can choose who deserves to experience this gift.

Be easy on yourself, I know you want to try to be perfect, but life is a journey and things will happen the way they are meant to happen. When you let go and let the creator take over, amazing things will happen, amazingness will be revealed! Remember to take care of yourself, remember to breathe and really take the time to relax. Cook good, healthy food for yourself, have days where you tidy up your space and really make sure your home is comfortable and neat, this will make you feel amazing! Also be easy on your loved ones, for everyone is on their own journey and each journey has its own, unique challenges, the best thing that you can do is just be there for them, nurture their soul and try to put yourself into their shoes once in a while. You have all the gifts right inside of you, I know you will find them and you will learn to truly love yourself the way that I love you.

Young Ones; Remember, You Are Young Once

By Michelle Malla *(Arviat, Nunavut)*

Live Boldly.

Feel Extremely.

Learn Intensely.

Explore Eagerly.

It is all based on what perspective you have towards your journey
in life.

Being content with who you are and what you have as you go
along in life is important.

Take it a step at a time, tippy toe if you have to, one day at a time.

Life gives you many avenues to practice, learn and grow.

Recognize.

Live.

Feel.

Learn.

Explore.

Dear Truth

By Mika Lafond

(Home: Muskeg Lake Cree Nation | Current: Treaty Six Territory)

I've been looking for you

all my life

trying to figure out

where I'm supposed to go.

I couldn't find you

so I tried to make it on my own

I thought all this time

if I was great

I would find my way.

But along life's path

I must have taken a wrong turn

because I'm lost

puzzled and unhappy

I'm torn between what I want

and what is

Stop the passing moons

for just one moment

find me

and help me

I need to make this step

back on my way again.

Truth, take my hand

and guide me through the day

It's Times Like This

By Mika Lafond

(Home: Muskeg Lake Cree Nation | Current: Treaty Six Territory)

woke up again last night

found myself alone in the dark

keep thinking my luck will change

and that I'll make my mark

gotta find the motivation

gotta find a little spark

getting caught up in the thinking

while this whole life falls apart

                         it's times like this when I turn the music on

                               just to hear another voice

                 and then I like to sing along just to hear my own

getting up this morning

crawling outta bed

same old story, same old life

nothing moving me ahead

people always rushing by

living the lives they wanted

and here I am breaking down

thoughts spinning in my head

it's times like this when I turn the music on

just to hear another voice

and then I like to sing along just to hear my own

all day long people are talking

just talking about themselves

I get lost in thought

dreaming 'bout love and wealth

I want to break my silence

I need to ask for help

but my eyes stay on the ground

too scared to push myself

it's times like this when I turn the music on

just to hear another voice

and then I like to sing along just to hear my own

I'm not asking for your judgment

so don't cast the first stone

going to get up tomorrow

going to pick up that phone

I'll reach for a dream

I'll stop being alone

got to get on life's road

make a path of my own

and it's not enough anymore when I turn the music on just to hear
another voice and I don't have to sing along

just to hear my own

Unstoppable

By Mika Lafond

(Home: Muskeg Lake Cree Nation | Current: Treaty Six Territory)

nôhkom tells stories of a fight for identity

she begins with a story about children

      missing children

      stolen children

children never returned

whole families fell deaf to the sound of a heart-spun language

prayers dampened by grief

voices bottled in confusion

each twisted thought formed by anger

and a people slammed in condemnation

the ones who took the children

told them

you are not who you are

missing children

      stolen children

forbidden to feel lost

demanded to erase all ties to home

at night

stars gazed upon weeping souls in dark rooms

children with hands pressed to their ears to block out the screams

terrified children

who whispered behind locked doors

I miss my mother

you are not who you are

they told the children

      frightened children

      dying children

nôhkom tells stories of a fight for identity

she says take it back for the children

throw dirt on the flames of privilege

smother the unkind ego

drench this night in lullabies

reclaim the ancient songs

raise your voices in revolution

return to the light of morning

give us back our children

this night of grief ends now

when a galaxy echoes with hundreds of thousands of voices exclaiming

I am who I am

an unstoppable spirit

Still Here

By Mika Lafond

(Home: Muskeg Lake Cree Nation | Current: Treaty Six Territory)

I love hip hop

I love the drum

It's all about heart

deep down the pulse in the music

brings the rhythm of change

rolling like thunder through my body

I love hip hop

I love the drum

because it's all about heart

on the outside I might be crying

the flow of the song

washes away the pain

cleaning the mess that is my life

Listen,

Remember the beat of real love

Your mother's heart

It's all you heard in the beginning

one beat, one heart, one love

I love hip hop

I love the drum

Living is all about heart

and the music is calling my name

reminding me

I'm still here.

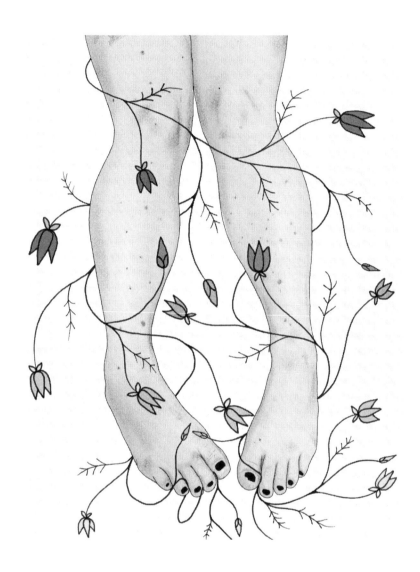

Remember This

By Aura *(Onyota'a:ka)*

Remember This

By Aura *(Onyota'a:ka)*

Bare skin

No shoes

Or socks

Open wounds

And old scars

Dirty soles

And callused heels

I am vulnerable and raw

But this time it's my choice

I'm done sweating my ass off in the summer heat

Ive been exposing my skin more over the last few days than the last several years of my life

As I look down at my legs, I can see all the dark brown, purple and red spots

They try to make their way up my entire body

Invading my all of my sacredness

I see people staring

Wondering what the fuck happened to me

The stories of pain are written all over my skin

Deeply engrained

There's no hiding the shame

I'm trying so hard to let go of it

But it clings to me like silk.

I call them constellations of scars

They come from stories of survival and resilience

These scars saved my life

When you look at my legs wondering what happened to me

Remember this

Identity

By Aura *(Onyota'a:ka)*

nineteen ninety eight denied, not enough

two thousand and one, lack of information

two thousand and eight, too much

two thousand and eleven, revision

two thousand and twelve denied, enfranchisement

two thousand and eighteen...

Imagine someone tries to take your identity away and give you land and money

Imagine they call this voluntary

Imagine that this leads to no longer having an identity

Imagine that your children won't know their culture or their language

Imagine they take your seven children away

Imagine turning to substances to take this pain away

Imagine having your life taken by the hands of another's

Imagine not knowing your children

Imagine not knowing your father

Imagine not knowing your mother

Imagine having to call strangers your family

Imagine how all of this will affect your grandchildren

Imagine having to apply to obtain your identity

Imagine being denied every time

Imagine you are either too much, or not enough

Imagine struggling to find a place to belong

Aaquaqsaq

By kivvaq (Nikita Larter) *(Home: Inuuvik, NT | Current: Tkaronto)*

Kwe Lessons

By Peyton Straker *(Home: Bear Clan from Keeseekoose First*

Nation, raised in Somba K'e, Denendeh | Current: Vancouver, BC)

Braid your life into medicine

Eat blackberries who grow wild along city streets

Learn to bead with two needles

Learn to bead with one

Gut the fish your own way

Shoot a moose with your own gun

The way your Setsuné would

Stretch sinew through your teeth

Scrape hide until moon time

Eat dry meat that you pounded yourself

Powwow braid your black silky lengths

Lick sticky spruce gum off your fingertips

Burn chaga under full moon

The way your Nokomis would

Sprinkle tobacco in new waters

Plant feet on new soil

Tell your white friends not to whistle at night

Shut your blinds before dusk

Pick fireweed in the fall

Pick bush tea to boil over fire

The way your Setsuné would

Throw your head back in laughter with your Sisters from all directions

Ask them where they got their earrings

Cry to Creator when your first queer Dene love breaks your heart

Ask Her for help

Tell Her you need the land to heal you

Tell Her thank you when the land heals you

The way your Nokomis would

Wear lipstick in the bush

Match your lipstick to your hanky

Flesh hide with painted nails

Pick the dry moose flesh bits off your dress

Wear your brain tan smoke smell proudly

Remember that every step you take in your slippers is resistance

The way your Setsuné would

Traumatic Resilience

By Sadie-Phoenix Lavoie *(Sagkeeng Anishinaabe Nation)*

You have all the reasons to not get up in the morning

And you know that you can break any second

With a simple trigger to set you off

Deeper than you have before

Afraid of what seems to be inevitable

Trauma always knocking on your door

Waiting to come in and refusing to leave

Worried that no one can hear your silent screams

And so you dwell on what should have happened

What you could have avoided

What would make life easier

But never did

Knowing it was out of your control

So you blame yourself for not being lucky

In a world that tells you that if you just worked hard enough

Was smart enough

Was cool enough

There may be a chance that you deserved a privilege key

To unlock the box of ignorance

But the universe doesn't work for you in that way

So you think karmas at fault from that fateful day

When there was that someone there to say

I don't want to go away

But you keep that chapter hidden

As if it will be gone for good ridden

Poking at you all of a sudden

Too much has been released

Taken innocence

So all you can do is reminisce

Of happier days of existence

It becomes too much to bare

When that's all you can stare

Knowing trauma is never fair

So you wish upon that blurry star

That someday you can reach that far

Away from the hurt you can no longer bare

Aching Bones from the gravity

Holding you close to reality

Forcing you to see

The universe for all it was meant to be

Accept life will be forever changed

Chapters constantly being rearranged

Book a never ending cage

So you burn it to stay warm

Setting off the fire alarm

Emergency crew suddenly arrives

Asking a billion questions at how you survived

So you ask yourself

Am I still alive?

Because you know

a piece of you died

Not sure if the rest rot away

as it was still tied

Compassion became the quickest medicine

friendship was what was missing

No need to hold it in

Hands now hold this blessing

Your past no longer an unbreakable seal

The future based on the cards you deal

The possibility to heal

That's all you ever want to feel

No longer the uncontrollable force

Just how you set your courses

So you look again and see

You are all you need to be

Resiliently Free

Unresolved

By Brenda Royal *(Blackfoot from Siksika First Nation)*

Systematic causes creating questions of pain as time pauses, our women and girls are sacred! The life givers lives are being taken by hatred! The calls of action are screaming across the land, Indigenous families want answers but no acknowledgement is ever given to the Indigenous man. Dear National Inquiry, you are investigating causes while working within a delegated time frame. I raise my middle finger to the mandate, you will never put a price on our Indigenous sister's names. I am a voice who is seeking the truth, when will they stop the violence that is placing my sisters in a box? I will never give up on those who are missing, I will keep searching for my sisters in my red moccs. A 15-year-old girl, whose body was found in the Red River, the verdict? "NOT GUILTY" of second degree murder! Where is the justice for our Indigenous children? "Reconciliation" is a joke, you can't be sorry when you're still continuing the same pattern. Dear Canada, genocide is still alive as it seems… but I will fight the good fight, for I am my Ancestors dreams.

Status Savage

By Brenda Royal *(Blackfoot from Siksika First Nation)*

I'm Statistically Hoping

By Alexandra Jarrett

(Canoe Lake Cree First Nation, Treaty 10 Territory)

In vulnerable hearts we will find our compassion that

will lead us to find restoration.

The following photos were created in collaboration with Indigenous Designer Dene Couture. She created these red dresses to honor those who have been lost to the #mmiw #mmim crisis. The Red Dress Project originated with Jamie Black who hung red dresses in forests and spaces in honor of those who have been lost. It is her exhibit that has inspired so many Indigenous women to take back their power. Red has become a symbol for our resilience and our ability to keep rising. In Cree the word for fire is **ᐃᐣᑯᐤ iskotew** and the word for woman is **ᐃᐣᑫᐤ iskwew** I believe it is our fire that will heal our people. Our women will lead, because we are blessed with intuition and the capacity to have compassion beyond ourselves. We must first practise compassion and love for self.

Red Dress Shoot Collaboration with Dene Couture,

Designer of Six Red Beads.

Hair: *Trisha Gardypie & Myrna Durocher.* **Makeup:** *Kehiew Fox, April Moosomin.* **Models:** *Chelsey Powder, Kyarra Sumners Daniels, Kyanna Desjarlais, Kehiew Fox, Kenisha McAdams, Rodrick Rabbitskin*

"If we all contribute in learning a piece of our Culture to Pass down,

then we can guarantee the Preservation of all Cultures"

- Dene Couture

If you could provide a message to the younger version of yourself to get through school, life, and challenging circumstances, what would you say?

I hope for a future where all youth realize their potential. I wish that they learn to nurture their talents and seek out what inspires them. Our youth are quite literally the future and they will have a lot of circumstances to rise above. These are my prayers for our youth.

You will find your tribe and if you can't find them immediately understand that you will find them eventually. Your happiness depends upon actively pursuing your bucket list. Focus on building yourself with compassion and integrity, your character depends on it. Chase your creativity and be relentless in learning your own form of art. Balance yourself in 4 ways emotionally, mentally, physically and spiritually. Decide what's important for you in these 4 areas at a young age and you will adjust better to your challenges. The better balanced you are the less power your circumstances will have over you.

"An entrepreneurial spirit is a sacred thing and should be treated as such. It can be scary to have a vision for your life, but the results will far outweigh your fears."

"In a picturesque view im a graphical delinquency a mother, a student a minor negativity. To the contrary I'm driven ambition. The world needs some heroes and I feel I'm solution."

- Alexandra Jarrett

As We Always Have

By Nicole Ineese-Nash (Songe Winnishe wabigwanikwe)

(Home: Constance Lake First Nation | Current: Tkaronto)

We exist not in the shadows of the unknown

But in the light of the possible

We flow

Leaving parts of ourselves in the emptiness

But we are not the vessel

We are the spaces between

We are the rivers

We overflow until there is no telling where one of us ends

and another begins

We are water

We are movement

We are together, collective and whole

We fit into roles that do not define us

We know ourselves

We are more

We are earth

We are stars

We cannot be proven or erased

We just are

And always will be

What Dreams Are Made Of

By Alicia BigCanoe *(Community: Chippewas of Georgina*

Island First Nation | Current: Tkaronto)

What Dreams Are Made Of

By Alicia BigCanoe *(Community: Chippewas of Georgina Island First Nation | Current: Tkaronto)*

What Dreams Are Made Of is inspired by reflecting back on the sacredness of my youth; a time of trial and error; a time where my ability to dream and connect with the spirit whirl was all that would carry me through the dark and confusing times.

My teen years were a struggle, searching for my birth mother on the streets of Toronto. Through graffiti stricken alley's and run-down buildings, and getting spiritually lost on the notorious corner of Bathurst and Queen Street in Toronto. Looking for a sense of connection but became further cut-off along the way. I wanted so badly to understand where I came from and why there was such an insurmountable void in my identity as an adopted half-native kid who grew up in Rexdale. A kid who had big dreams, but nothing to work from but a first name and my imagination.

When I finally did find her, I wasn't prepared for what was in store. The more I learned, the more I became the next person in our bloodline tasked with taking on inter-generations of trauma and fight for survival. I came to a place here my heart was over-flowing with grief and sadness, yet I was yearning for healing, connection, and love.

After many failed attempts to move the energy inside of me, I started to weave dream catchers, write, bead, and then paint.

Finding art as a channel to healing, I fade into my open canvases that await me. In these moments I like to create because it grounds me and helps my spirit fly.

So I step back and dip my brushes into stories of the past/present/future and weave my emotions through dream-catching webs of freedom.

To my inner-youth, and youth today; you are worth every ounce of love that you can give yourself. Keep trying, and you are not alone. Talk to someone if you are struggling with something; there are a lot of people out there who care about your well-being. Future generations will thank you for pushing through this crazy web we call life.

Dream well.

Mechanics of Creation

By Alicia BigCanoe *(Community: Chippewas of Georgina*

Island First Nation | Current: Tkaronto)

89

Ending Stigma

By Regional Chief Kluane Adamek *(Home: Kluane First Nation*

Current: Whitehorse, YK)

Talking about our struggles with mental wellness can be incredibly difficult. While it is so common for many of us to work through a mental health challenge at some point in our lives, we don't always talk openly about issues like depression and self-harm. This is why ending the stigma around mental health is critical.

I encourage everyone to remember that mental awareness is a journey we are all undertaking.

The Person That You Have Dreamed of Becoming

By Jacey Firth-Hagen

(Home: Inuvik, Northwest Territories | Current: Edmonton, AB)

I love you. We need you here. You are important, amazing, beautiful, strong, smart and loved. You are worthy of all things good, don't ever doubt that. You'll get through it, just keep going no matter how hard it may seem. Be easy on yourself, no matter what you may be going through. What I want you to know is that it's okay to not be okay. You can do anything that you put your mind to. Believe in yourself, things will get better. It's okay to share what you are feeling. It's okay to feel happy and to love yourself. A lot of things may not make sense but maybe they aren't supposed to, that's okay to. Going through tough times I often dreamed about learning my language, being out on the land, caribou hunting, graduating High School, travelling the country, and seeing the world. I still keep that vision of myself to this day. I envision myself graduating, successful, happy, and travelling on the land and throughout cities. I never let that dream go. I want you to know that it is possible to be all that you can dream and to work towards that dream, follow your heart. Life is not a race, and it's okay

to take things at your own pace. Even if it is just by a second, minute,

hour, day, month, or year at a time. No matter how long it takes, don't

give up. To the shy, confused, hurt, angry, girl with the low self-esteem

just trying to get through the day; I love you, I forgive you, thank you.

Love,

The Person That You Have Dreamed of Becoming

Imperfect Clay

By Destiny Rae *(Tkaronto)*

Perfection.

An idealistic notion.

The embodiment of a fairytale...

The exclusion of all flaws

All cracks

All "broken-ness".

Alas it is the perfect illusion

For with perfection

Comes the prospect of fragility

The desperate need to maintain its pristine form

The perfect form

The perfect way

But how then does the light

Break through...

If nothing is broken?

If there are no cracks n crevices for it to peek through

And fill with its warmth

That cold, hard, perfection.

What's it worth?

So afraid to be damaged...

To try to be something different

Try something new

To grow

To change

Why change what's already perfect?

It already is.

It....just.... is.

What it is.

Plain. Simple. Perfect.

No ridges to rise...

Like the sun or the plates the earth holds inside

The ones that break free from the soil

Towards the sky

The mountains

The birds

The natural high

Why?

Do we chase this thing that is so stagnant?

My question is for you

The pressures you place on your greatness

The scrutiny in everything you do

Yes. You are imperfect.

But to refuse that is to refuse your gift

See the gold lining on your cracks

Acknowledge the beauty that you missed

There's a seed inside of you

That's longing to grow

But it needs food

And it needs light

And it needs you to know

That it is all imperfect

This thing we call life

But there is the beauty

Between all the laughter n all the strife

We are not meant to be perfect

For then there would be nothing to heal

That cold hard perfection

Tell me how then you could feel?

Two Children

By Evelyn Pakinewatik *(Home: Nipissing First Nation*

Current: Scarborough, ON)

Two children visit me.

One is a son, myself. The child who was brilliant, and angry, and

loving. She chased down other children with teeth bared and threw

her first punch when she learned that she could meet any challenge.

She would climb any tree, wall, or doorframe. She read everything

she could hold and was confident she could oversee the delivery of a

healthy baby by the time she was 10. She knew how it worked - all of it.

Birth, the body, its many moving parts. I trashed many sketchbooks

filled with her anatomical studies. She understood time and she saw

how little it was, the thinnest sticky film clinging to reality. A deck of

cards in different breaths. She lived in the water but was made of fire,

and was always surrounded by steam and smoke. She saw spirits until

they became demons and sent them away with fear on her tongue. She

saw lightning and loved thunder. Rain brought her comfort. I believed

for years that she had died, but she hadn't; and I am forgiving her all of her foolishness and wrath. I forgive her of her bad decisions. I forgot so much of her after the grey rotted away and grew again, but she is coming back to me, and to the life that we have shared.

The other is a daughter, my daughter, as yet unborn and waiting. I spend half my tears crying for a future where she is not living, but she says will find me when I am ready. She is exactly what we hoped for, and more, she carries strength and wisdom and she is perfectly beautiful and whole. We do not take from her as we were taken from. We give. She gives. I know her love already, even if it is only in the form of a dream. One day she will tell me her name, and it will carry real, tangible power. I am not waiting for her, but I look forward to her, and one day I will build her regalia in vibrant dream colors; electric and bold. She is medicine. I look at her eyes and see my ancestors and all their warrior blood. I look at her and I see water.

Two children visit me. One informs the other. Both are shaped by dreams. Both are shaped by stories.

And I love them.

Everything happens when it is meant to.

To My Younger Self

By Erica Lugt *(Home: Tuktoyaktuk, NT*

Current: Beaufort Delta Region, Inuvik)

What I would tell my younger self? Because I came from an abusive home what I would love to have been told or known is that if you are ever feeling frustrated with life, there are resources out there for you. Basically you are not as alone as you may think you are! Look for someone or something that allows you to feel the support & love that you need to get you through your tough times (I read books on forgiveness, spirituality & I create). Rise above your struggles and remember we are always capable of changing our own thoughts & our surroundings. Don't let being a victim consume your identity. I will use myself as an example, "my mom beat me everyday of my childhood but instead of taking that and being angry and letting it define who I am and consuming that victim role, I chose to be a better person, the way I see life....everyday is a new day to be a better person than you were yesterday, and I chose to walk forward with a loving heart, creating & always learning, I learned that my mom also had a rough childhood, it does not excuse her behaviour but I also understood it was not me, it was never my fault, it was about her and her struggles"

I love my mom! I forgave her!

Healing Journey:

For me, I found great joy in what I do, which is I create earrings with beads. The love of beading has helped me to believe in myself, it has pushed me and continues to help me towards being my highest self. My world changed with this new hobby of mine. People started to see that in my work and the support started flooding in. I have had many amazing opportunities land my way because of beading so if I can help you in any way. I would like to say, I was once you and I would like to suggest finding a healthy hobby. Find ways to create that fits your wants and that satisfies your soul to help you get through your tough times. Creating creates such positive energy! To put art into this world is the most satisfying feeling! ....and remember, art comes in many forms!! Seriously anytime my energy is low I take to my beads and always put the needle down with a more clear vision than before I sat down. Find your passion!